W9-BIU-805

BACKYARD ANIMALS

SQUIRRELS

by Wendy Strobel Dieker

AMICUS | AMICUS INK

claws

teeth

Look for these
words and pictures
as you read.

tail

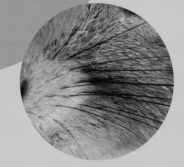

whiskers

What is in the tree?
It is a squirrel.

teeth

Squirrels are rodents.
They have long front teeth.

Look at its bushy tail.
It gives shade in the summer.
It keeps him warm in the winter.

tail

claws

Look at its claws.

Its claws help it climb.

It climbs on trees and fence posts.

Look at its big eyes.
A squirrel sees well.
It watches for enemies.

Look at its whiskers.
These hairs feel the ground.
They feel for food.

whiskers

The squirrel found a nut!
It will hide the nut.
In winter, it will have food.

claws

Look at its claws.
Its claws help it climb.
It climbs on trees and fence posts.

teeth

Squirrels are rodents.
They have long front teeth.

claws

teeth

Did you find?

tail

whiskers

Look at its bushy tail.
It gives shade in the summer.
It keeps him warm in the winter.

tail

Look at its whiskers.
These hairs feel the ground.
They feel for food.

whiskers

Spot is published by Amicus and Amicus Ink
P.O. Box 1329, Mankato, MN 56002
www.amicuspublishing.us

Library of Congress Cataloging-in-Publication Data
Names: Dieker, Wendy Strobel, author.
Title: Squirrels / by Wendy Strobel Dieker.
Description: Mankato, Minnesota : Amicus, [2018] | Series:
  Spot. Backyard animals | Audience: Grade K-3.
Identifiers: LCCN 2016044420 (print) | LCCN 2017000864
  (ebook) | ISBN 9781681510972 (library binding) | ISBN
  9781681511870 (e-book) | ISBN 9781681522227 (pbk.)
Subjects: LCSH: Squirrels--Juvenile literature.
Classification: LCC QL737.R68 D54 2018 (print) | LCC
  QL737.R68 (ebook) | DDC 599.36--dc23
LC record available at https://lccn.loc.gov/2016044420

Printed in the United States of America

HC 10 9 8 7 6 5 4 3 2 1
PB 10 9 8 7 6 5 4 3 2 1

Rebecca Glaser, editor
Deb Miner, series designer
Ciara Beitlich, book designer
Holly Young, photo researcher

All photos by Shutterstock except:
Alamy, 2, 12–13, 15; iStock 2, 8–9,
10–11, 15

SQUIRRELS